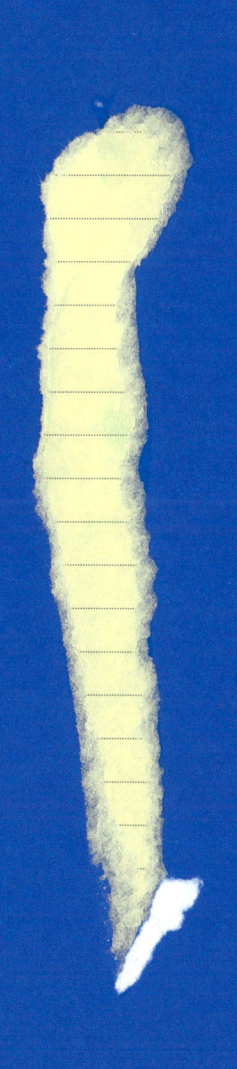

Cities Through Time

London

A photographic exploration of how the city has developed and changed

ANNE ROONEY

Chrysalis Children's Books

First published in the UK in 2005 by
Chrysalis Children's Books
An imprint of Chrysalis Books Group Plc
The Chrysalis Building, Bramley Road,
London W10 6SP

Copyright © Chrysalis Books Group Plc 2005

All rights reserved. No part of this book may be reproduced or utilised in any form or by any means, electronic or mechanical, including photocopying, recording or by any information storage and retrieval system, without permission in writing from the publisher, except by a reviewer who may quote brief passages in a review.

ISBN 1 84458 355 4

British Library Cataloguing in Publication Data for this book is available from the British Library.

Anne Rooney has asserted her right under the Copyright, Design and Patents Act 1988 to be identified as the author of this work.

Contact Anne Rooney by e-mail (anne@annerooney.co.uk) or visit her website (www.annerooney.co.uk).

Associate Publisher Joyce Bentley
Editorial Manager Rasha Elsaeed
Project Editor Leon Gray
Editorial Assistant Camilla Lloyd
Consultant Jeff Lewis
Designer Alix Wood
Illustrator Mark Walker
Picture Researcher Jamie Dikomite

Printed in China

10 9 8 7 6 5 4 3 2 1

Read Regular, READ SMALLCAPS and Read Space;
European Community Design Registration 2003
and Copyright © Natascha Frensch 2001-2004
Read Medium, Read Black and Read Slanted
Copyright © Natascha Frensch 2003-2004

READ™ is a revolutionary new typeface that will enhance children's understanding through clear, easily recognisable character shapes. With its evenly spaced and carefully designed characters, READ™ will help children at all stages to improve their literacy skills, and is ideal for young readers, reluctant readers and especially children with dyslexia.

Picture Acknowledgments
All reasonable efforts have been made to ensure the reproduction of content has been done with the consent of copyright owners. If you are aware of any unintentional omissions please contact the publishers directly so that any necessary corrections may be made for future editions.

T=Top, B=Bottom, L=Left, R=Right, C=Centre
Antiquarian Images: 5T
Chrysalis Image Library: 6, 14B
Corbis: 1, 21 London Aerial Photo Library; 20T Bettmann Corporation of London, London Metropolitan Archives: 14T
English Heritage/National Monuments Record: FC B, 10B, 16B, 22, 24T, 24B, 26T, 26B, 28C, 28B
Guildhall Library, Corporation of London: 12T
Getty Images: FC C; 20B Hulton Archive; 25B Joe Cornish
Memories: FC TL, BC TL, BC C, 8, 10T, 12B, 16T
Museum of London: 4, 18, 28T
Rex Features: 17T Peter MacDiarmid; 19T Tony Kyriacou
Science Photo Library: 5B NASA
Simon Clay/Chrysalis Image Library: FC TR, BC TR, 2, 3, 7T, 7B, 9, 11T, 11B, 13T, 13B, 15T, 15B, 17B, 19B, 23, 25T, 27T, 27B, 29TL, 29TR, 29B, 31

CONTENTS

Welcome to London 4
Cityscape 6
Remembering History 8
Streets and Traffic 10
Markets 12
The River 14
Bridges 16
Royal London 18
The Blitz 20
Crime and Punishment 22
Public Spaces 24
All Change 26
No Change 28
Find out More 30
Glossary 31
Index 32

WELCOME TO LONDON

The Romans founded the first permanent settlement in London around 50 CE. Early Roman engineers built a wooden bridge over the River Thames and a town grew up around it. London has grown into the second largest city in Europe, after Moscow in Russia.

Then and now

Throughout its long history, London has suffered many natural and human-made disasters, including outbreaks of plague, the Great Fire of 1666, bombing raids, riots and terrorist attacks.

During the Blitz of World War II (1939–1945), German bombers devastated London, and many important buildings were destroyed. Young children who lived in London were evacuated to the safety of the countryside, while their parents carried on living and working in the city.

Today, London is home to the Royal Family and the Houses of Parliament, and the city is the capital of England.

Piccadilly Circus, late 1890s

Time line

43–50 CE First settlement in London by the Romans

61 CE London burns during a rebellion led by Boudicca's army

200 CE London becomes the capital of southern England; city walls are built

457–600 Change from Roman city to a Saxon trading town

800s Sacked and burned by Vikings

883 King Alfred drives the Vikings out of England

1066 England falls to Norman French at the Battle of Hastings

1176–1209 Stone London Bridge built over the River Thames

The population of London has grown from 30,000 in 250 CE to 7 million in 2000

How to use this book

In this book you will find photos of London as it was in the past and as it is now. There are questions about the photos to get you to look at and think about them carefully. You may need to do some research to answer some of the questions. You might be able to use:

- encyclopaedias
- CD-ROMs
- reference books
- the Internet.

Page 30 lists useful websites and some films you might like to watch, which show London at different times.

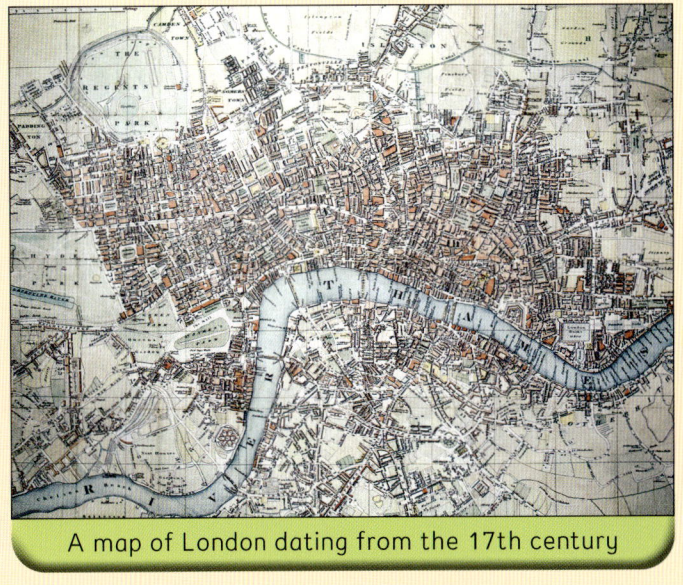

A modern satellite image of London

A map of London dating from the 17th century

1348–1349 Black Death kills 60 per cent of the population of London

1665 Great Plague kills 70,000 people

1750 Second bridge built over the River Thames

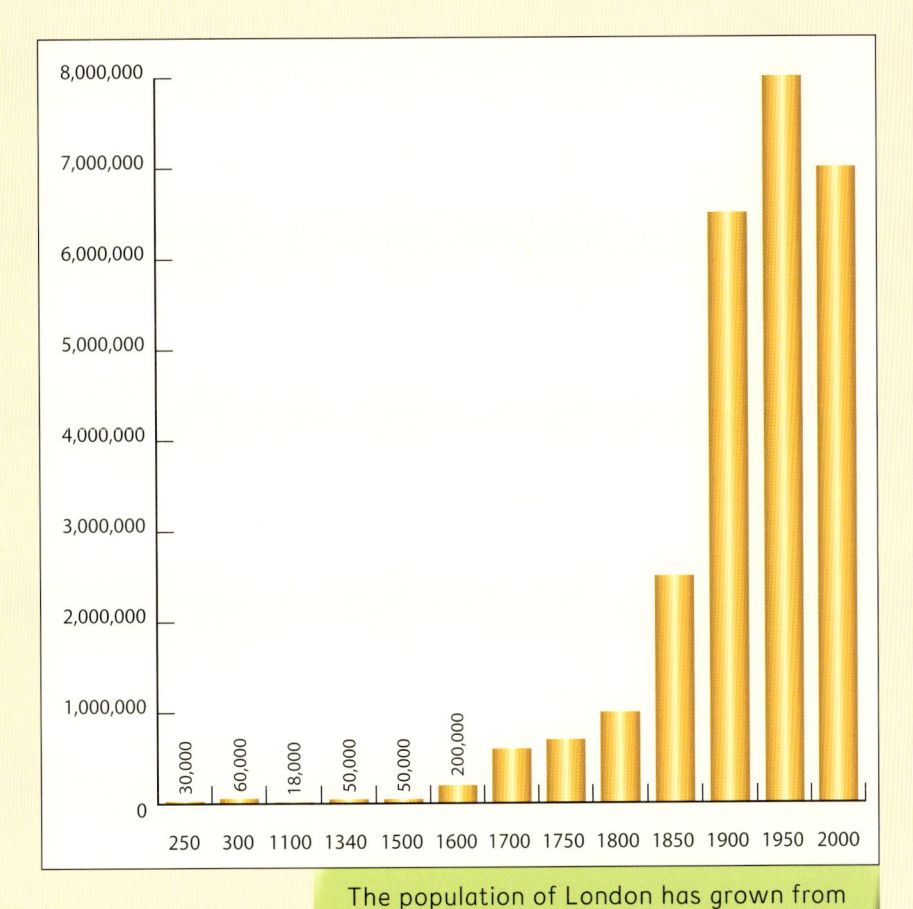

1853 The Great Stink: The River Thames is so polluted that the London sewer system is built

2000 Millennium Dome is built in Greenwich

1400 England's parliament fixed in London

1666 Great Fire destroys most of London

1848–1849 Cholera epidemic kills many people in London

1939–1945 The Blitz: London suffers at the hands of German bombers during World War II

CITYSCAPE

A view over a city from a height can reveal whether the city has tall or short buildings, whether there are green spaces, how crowded it is and whether it is flat or hilly. London is relatively flat with lots of green spaces. Historically, the city has always been densely populated. If London continues to grow, more and more tall buildings will appear.

Back in time

- What is the main type of tall building you can see in the old photo taken from St Mary le Bow below?
- What type of tall buildings can you see in the new photo on the opposite page?
- What other types of buildings can you see in the older photo? Are there any buildings like this in the new photo?
- What can you see happening at the upper left and centre of the new photo taken from St Mary le Bow? How might this affect the skyline?

View from St Mary le Bow

Building up

Many new buildings have been put up in London in recent years. You can see some on the skyline of the recent photo taken from St Mary le Bow and also in the photo of Greenwich.

- What do you think these buildings will be used for? Will people live in them?
- The street on the left of the photos of St Mary le Bow is called Cheapside. It used to be lined with shops. Today, many people work in Cheapside, but few live nearby. What kinds of shops do you think you would find there today?

Investigate

Visit a high place, such as a tall building or a hill, where you can look down on the area where you live. What type of buildings or features can you see? Draw a picture of the scene. Your picture does not need to be very detailed, but it should show clearly the buildings that are most noticeable, such as, office blocks, a church or a large hospital. Make sure you include any lakes, parks, rivers or other natural features that break up the scene.

View from St Mary le Bow

Inset: The skyline at Greenwich

REMEMBERING HISTORY

On 2 September 1666, a fire started in a bakery in Pudding Lane. The fire spread rapidly. It raged for several days and destroyed most of London. At the time, most buildings were made of wood and were built close together. This helped the fire to spread. Many important buildings were destroyed in the Great Fire, but historians think that not many people were killed.

Monument to the fire

Sir Christopher Wren and Robert Hook designed the Monument to commemorate the Great Fire of London. It was built close to where the fire started.

- Compare the two photos of the Monument. How has the area around the Monument changed since the earlier photo was taken? Why do you think this is?
- How has the Monument itself changed?
- In 1666, many bakers worked in the area where the Monument now stands. Look at the recent photo. Can you tell how it is used now? What sort of buildings can you see?

Monument to the Great Fire of London, c.1920

Memorials

Memorials are often built to commemorate historic events. Some memorials are statues or columns similar to the Monument. Others serve a useful purpose, such as bridges or parks.

- Do you think memorials help people remember past events?
- Does it make a difference whether or not a memorial serves a useful purpose?
- Is there a monument near you? Find out more about it. What does it commemorate?

Disaster strikes

Fire is one of several types of disasters that can destroy a city.

- Can you think of other types of disasters that can have such a devastating effect on a city? Have you heard about any recent disasters? What effect do they have on the people living in a city?

Investigate

An English writer called Samuel Pepys watched the Great Fire and wrote down what he saw in his diary. Imagine that you were living in London during the Great Fire and had to leave your home to escape. What would it have been like? Write your own diary entry explaining what you did and how you felt.

Monument to the Great Fire of London

STREETS AND TRAFFIC

The street scenes depicted in the photos on these two pages were taken in Bishopsgate and High Holborn in the centre of London. Both have been busy streets for a very long time – Bishopsgate since Roman times, and Holborn since the Middle Ages. Bishopsgate once had large houses in which rich merchants lived. Today, both streets are business districts.

Bishopsgate, c.1920

High Holborn, 1890

Life on the street

- What types of vehicles can you see in the old and new photos of Bishopsgate and High Holborn? What are they being used for?
- Look at the two photos of Bishopsgate. How are the buses different in the photos?
- Look at the pedestrians in the old and new photos. What is different about their clothes and what they are doing?
- How have the two streets themselves changed? Look at the street furniture, such as road signs, lighting and markings on the roads.
- Do the streets in your local area look similar to the recent photos of Bishopsgate and High Holborn? If not, how do they differ?

City congestion

There is a lot of traffic on the streets in both the early and recent photos. In the early photo of Holborn, the carriages and carts are being pulled along by horses. In Victorian times, people worried that if horse-drawn traffic increased even more, there would be too much horse manure on the streets, and London would be unable to cope with the pollution.

- How does traffic cause problems on city streets today? What types of pollution are caused by road traffic?
- What other methods of transport do people use in modern cities? Are these methods better for the environment?

Bishopsgate

Investigate

Conduct a survey to find out how people in your class travel to school. Draw a bar chart to record your results. Which methods of transport do you think cause the most and the least pollution? Can you think of any other advantages and disadvantages to each method? Make a poster asking people to adopt environmentally friendly ways of travelling.

High Holborn

MARKETS

Cattle and later meat have been sold at Smithfield Market since the ninth century. In Victorian times, the area was a health hazard – full of blood, manure and bits of rotten meat. Today, Smithfield Market is clean and hygienic. Live cattle have not been sold in Smithfield Market since 1852.

Market life

Spitalfields Market sold fruit and vegetables to shops, restaurants and other traders from 1682 until 1991.

- What changes can you see in the two photos of Smithfield Market?
- Do you think Spitalfields Market looks different inside now from how it looked in Victorian times? How and why might it have changed?
- What are people selling in the earlier photo of Spitalfields Market? What are they selling in the recent photo?
- Do you live near a market? What can you buy there?

Spitalfields Market, 1954

Smithfield Market, c.1905

Food habits

Spitalfields used to be very dirty. Today, there are laws about how hygienic a place must be if it is used to sell or prepare food.

- Why do you think there are laws about markets and food today?
- What should you do to keep your food safe and clean?

People can now buy many different foods that were not available in Victorian times. Your family might do all the weekly shopping from one supermarket.

- Do you think a Victorian family would be able to buy all their food in one place? Why or why not?

Investigate

Imagine you lived in Victorian times. Find some old recipes, and plan meals for your family for the day. Write out your shopping list. Next to each item, say where you would need to buy it. Compare the list to what you eat now. Which foods can we buy now that a Victorian family could not buy?

Spitalfields Market

Smithfield Market

THE RIVER

Like many major cities, London is built along a river, called the Thames. For centuries, London was the greatest port in the world, and the River Thames linked the city to the sea and the world. Ships from all over the world transported necessities and luxuries to the very heart of the capital.

London lifeline

- What types of boats can you see in the photos on these two pages?
- What do you think people use the boats for now and what were they used for in the past?
- In what ways do people and goods move around London today?
- Why do you think cranes are useful in the West India Dock?

The Tower of London was built as a fortress in 1078. It has served many purposes, the most famous of which is as a prison.

- Why do you think it was built close to the river?

The River Thames at the Tower of London

West India Dock, 19th century

Using the river

The West India Dock was once used to unload goods that came to London from the West Indies.

- Where are the West Indies? Find out what sort of goods came to England from the West Indies. What do we get from the West Indies now? How do you think it gets here?

Today, people use rivers in many different ways.

- Is there a river near you? How do people use it? Do you think people would have done the same things a hundred years ago?

Investigate

Using a map of London, design an advertisement for a tourist boat trip along the River Thames. What will people see? Tell them about the landmarks along the way. Draw a map showing the route of the boat trip. You can find out lots of information about the famous landmarks along the River Thames from the websites listed on page 30.

The River Thames at the Tower of London

West India Dock

BRIDGES

The Romans built the first bridge over the River thames. It was made of wood. Construction of the first stone bridge started in 1176. Houses and shops were built along it, and the heads of executed criminals were displayed on spikes at the gateway at the end of the bridge. The old London Bridge in the photo below was built in 1831. It was taken apart in 1973 and rebuilt in Lake Havasu City in Arizona, America.

Tower Bridge

Building bridges

- Compare the two photos of London Bridge. How is the new London Bridge different from the old London Bridge? How are people crossing the bridge in the older photo?
- Find out about Tower Bridge. What is special about this bridge? Why was it built like this?
- Find out about the Millennium Bridge. What is special about this bridge?

Old London Bridge from Southwark

Millennium Bridge

Investigate

Find out about different types of bridges. Pick a river or a stream near where you live, and design a bridge to cross it. What type of bridge will it be? Will it be for pedestrians, traffic or both? What materials will it be made of? Make a model of your bridge.

Help or hindrance?

Many early settlers started their villages or towns near rivers. As more people settled along the river, they soon needed a way of crossing it.

- Why did people settle near rivers? How did people cross rivers before they could make bridges?

- In what ways do people cross rivers now instead of using bridges? Find out if the River Thames can be crossed in any of these ways in London.

- Not all bridges go over rivers. Find out how many bridges there are in your local area. Do they all cross rivers and streams? What else are bridges used for?

London Bridge

ROYAL LONDON

Buckingham Palace has served as the official residence of Britain's kings and queens since 1837. Although it is used for many official events and receptions, parts of Buckingham Palace are open to the public during August and September.

A royal residence

- How has the palace changed since the photo on this page was taken?
- Can you see the policemen by the gate and the soldiers in red jackets in the recent photo of Buckingham Palace? What job do you think they do?

The front of Buckingham Palace was refaced with Portland Stone by the English architect Sir Aston Webb in 1912.

- What else has been added to the front of Buckingham Palace? Do you prefer the old or the new style?

The British Royal Family often appears on the balcony at the front of the palace at occasions such as royal weddings.

- Why do you think the British Royal Family uses the balcony?

Buckingham Palace, before 1912

Investigate

Pick a tourist attraction, either that you know or that you would like to visit, and find out about it. Why is it interesting? Why do people like to go there? What can you do when you get there? How much does it cost to visit? When you have found out more about it, make a poster to advertise it to tourists.

Royal rulers

Britain is ruled by a king or queen, but it is also a democracy. In a democracy, the people vote for representatives, called politicians, to make all the decisions about how the country is run.

- Find out about two more countries that are ruled by a king or queen?

- Buckingham Palace is more than just a home for the British Royal Family. Find out what else it is used for.

Many tourists visit London to see Buckingham Palace and the Tower of London, which is home to the Crown Jewels. Royal events such as weddings, funerals and christenings are shown on television.

- Why do you think people are interested in the Royal Family?

Inset: Royals on the balcony

Buckingham Palace

THE BLITZ

During World War II (1939–1945), German bombers carried out raids on London in what has become known as the Blitz. Many people were killed, and important buildings destroyed. Young children were evacuated to the countryside to escape the danger. People who stayed in London were not allowed to switch on lights in their houses after dark. They built air-raid shelters, in which they hid during bombing raids. Those who had no air-raid shelter often hid in cellars or in the underground railway tunnels.

People shelter in the Underground during a bombing raid

St Paul's Cathedral, 1940

The Blitz

- Compare the old and recent photos of St Paul's Cathedral and the surrounding area. What major differences can you see?
- Can you find any buildings that look the same in both photos? What kind of buildings are they?
- What kind of buildings have been built where the bombed buildings once stood?
- Why did people shelter in the Underground during bombing raids? How are the people in the photo trying to make themselves comfortable?

Consequences of war

Many important buildings and homes were totally destroyed during the Blitz of World War II. London was not rebuilt until after the war had ended.

- Apart from the danger of the bombs, what problems do you think Londoners had to face during the war?

There were food shortages during and after World War II, so many people grew their own fruit and vegetables. Some foods were rationed. Each person was allowed a certain amount of butter, cheese, eggs, meat, milk, and sugar each week, and they could not buy any more than the ration allowed.

- What types of foods do you like to eat? How would you feel if you were only allowed a small amount of your favourite foods every week?

Investigate

Children who were evacuated to the country were sent away on a train without their parents. They had to live with people they had never met. Some stayed away from home for many years. Imagine that you have been evacuated during the Blitz. Write a letter to your parents in the city. Describe how you felt on the journey and what it is like to live among a strange family.

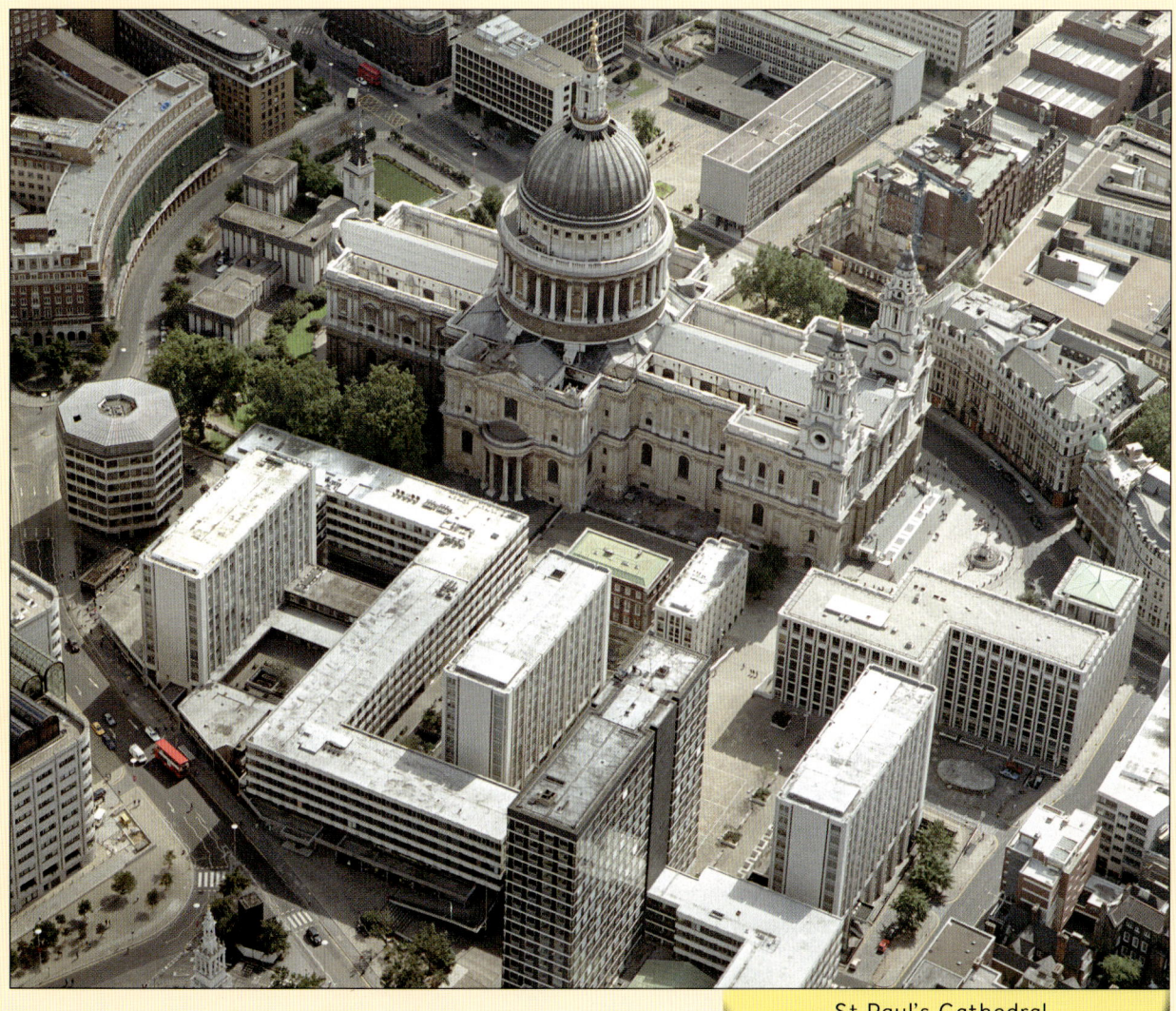

St Paul's Cathedral

CRIME AND PUNISHMENT

The Old Bailey is the central criminal court in London. Many infamous criminals have been tried and sentenced there since it opened in 1907. The Old Bailey contains the famous Courts 1 and 2, where some of the most shocking cases in criminal history have been heard.

Newgate Gaol

The Old Bailey was built on the site of the old Newgate Gaol. There had been a prison there since 1188. Newgate Gaol was built between 1773 and 1780 and demolished in 1902.

- Can you spot any similarities in the old photo of Newgate Gaol and the recent photo of the Old Bailey? Do the streets look any different?
- Have you seen any other buildings that have domes, columns, or statues on top? What types of buildings are they?
- Find out about the Statue of Justice on top of the Old Bailey. What is she holding? Why?
- Does Newgate Gaol look like you would expect a prison to look? How, if at all, is it different from your expectations?
- Why do you think there are no windows in Newgate Gaol?

Newgate Gaol

Rough justice

The conditions in Newgate Gaol used to be terrible. It was crowded, filthy and infested with rats. Many prisoners fell ill, and some died.

From 1783 to 1868, criminals were executed (killed for their crimes) outside Newgate Gaol where crowds could come to watch. People are no longer executed in the United Kingdom.

- Find out what people could be executed for in earlier times.
- What happens to people who commit crimes in Britain now?

Investigate

Elizabeth Fry was born in 1780. She visited Newgate Gaol in the early 19th century and was horrified by the terrible conditions in which the prisoners lived. She worked for them to be treated better. Find out what you can about Elizabeth Fry, and make a display with words and pictures. Imagine what it would have been like to be a prisoner in Newgate, and make up some quotations from prisoners to go in your display.

The Old Bailey

PUBLIC SPACES

Trafalgar Square and Hyde Park Corner are two important tourist attractions in the centre of London. They have been public meeting places for hundreds of years.

Hyde Park Corner, 1890s

Trafalgar Square, 1906

Meeting up

The area around Trafalgar Square has been an important public meeting place for Londoners since the 9th century. Tourists go to Trafalgar Square to feed the pigeons, see the statues and fountains and be photographed near Nelson's Column and the bronze lions. Hyde Park has been a public park since 1637. People go there to walk, exercise, roller blade, picnic, and row on the boating lake.

- How has Trafalgar Square changed since the old photo was taken?
- What are people doing in the recent photo of Trafalgar Square?
- How has Hyde Park Corner changed?
- How are people travelling to and around the park in the two photos of Hyde Park?
- Look at the people in all the photos on these two pages. What types of people do you think they are, and what are they doing?

Places for people

People go to both Hyde Park and Trafalgar Square for political meetings, to hear people speak about things that matter to them and for public events such as concerts, firework displays and parties.

- Is there a public space in your local area that is used like this? Find out about it. What do people do there? What kind of events take place?

Both Hyde Park and Trafalgar Square have several statues and memorials that commemorate important people or events.

- Do you know of any memorials or statues near your home? Why have they been put up?

Investigate

There are four plinths (stone blocks to support statues) at the corners of Trafalgar Square. Three of them have a statue, but the fourth stood empty for two hundred years. A fourth statue will soon be added. Design a statue that could go on the final plinth. Try to make it relevant to Trafalgar Square – perhaps to its history or to how it is used now.

Hyde Park Corner

Trafalgar Square

ALL CHANGE

Covent Garden was a market garden run by monks in the Middle Ages. Today, the area is full of cafés, entertainers and market stalls. In 1950, the Festival of Britain Exhibition was held on the South Bank. After the exhibition, all the new buildings in the area were demolished except for the Royal Festival Hall.

Changing places

- How do you think it would feel different in Covent Garden now compared to a hundred years ago?
- How has the South Bank area been changed? What do you think the buildings are used for in each photo?

Covent Garden Market, 19th century

Bankside, Southwark, 1946

Redevelopment

Some areas are completely redeveloped when the needs of a city change. In Covent Garden and the South Bank, working places have been transformed into places where people go to enjoy themselves.

- Is there an area near you that has changed completely? How is it used now and how was it used before?

The Globe Theatre is a replica of the theatre in which Shakespeare's plays were first performed during the late 16th and early 17th centuries. Find out more about life in Elizabethan London. What would you expect the Globe to be like in Elizabethan times?

Investigate

Imagine that you worked in Covent Garden as a child. You have now grown up with grandchildren of your own. You are sitting in a Covent Garden café writing a postcard to a childhood friend. Tell him or her about the changes to the area.

Covent Garden

South Bank: Tate Modern and the Globe Theatre

NO CHANGE

The George Inn was first built during the Middle Ages, but it was destroyed by a fire and rebuilt in 1676. The Palace of Westminster is the home of central government in Britain. Parliament has met in Westminster since the end of the 14th century. The Midland Grand Hotel was built next to St Pancras railway station in 1872. It closed in 1935. The building was used for offices and then left empty. It is now restored and has re-opened as a hotel.

George Inn, 1896

Big Ben and the Palace of Westminster, 1910

Midland Grand Hotel, St Pancras, after 1872

Old and new

- What differences can you see in the two photos of the George Inn? How would it be different to be a customer at the inn now?
- Can you see any differences in the old and recent photos of the Palace of Westminster and of the Grand Midland Hotel at St Pancras?
- How do you think these buildings might have changed inside?

George Inn

Restoration

Many old buildings are demolished and replaced with new buildings, but many others are restored. Sometimes they are used for the same purpose, and sometimes their use changes with time.

- How do you think the hotel changed when it was converted into offices?

There are many different reasons for restoring an old building.

- Make a list of some the reasons for restoring old buildings. Who do you think decides which buildings to restore and which ones to demolish?

Investigate

Choose an old building in your local area. Find out when it was built, what it was used for and how it has changed over the years. Has it always been used in the same way? Imagine that your local or school library is putting up a display about old buildings in the area. Make a display of materials for the building you have chosen.

Big Ben and the Palace of Westminster

St Pancras

FIND OUT MORE

On the map

This map shows where the places photographed in the book are in London.

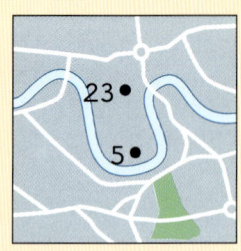

1. Bishopsgate (pages 10, 11)
2. Buckingham Palace (pages 18, 19)
3. Covent Garden (pages 26, 27)
4. George Inn (pages 28, 29)
5. Greenwich (page 7)
6. High Holborn (pages 10, 11)
7. Houses of Parliament (pages 28, 29)
8. Hyde Park Corner (pages 24, 25)
9. London Bridge (pages 16, 17)
10. Millennium Bridge (page 17)
11. Monument (pages 8, 9)
12. Old Bailey (page 23)
13. Piccadilly Circus (page 4)
14. St Mary le Bow (pages 6, 7)
15. St Pancras (pages 28, 29)
16. St Paul's Cathedral (pages 20, 21)
17. Smithfield Market (pages 12, 13)
18. South Bank (pages 26, 27)
19. Spitalfields Market (pages 12, 13)
20. Tower Bridge (page 16)
21. Tower of London (pages 14, 15)
22. Trafalgar Square (pages 24, 25)
23. West India Dock (pages 14, 15)

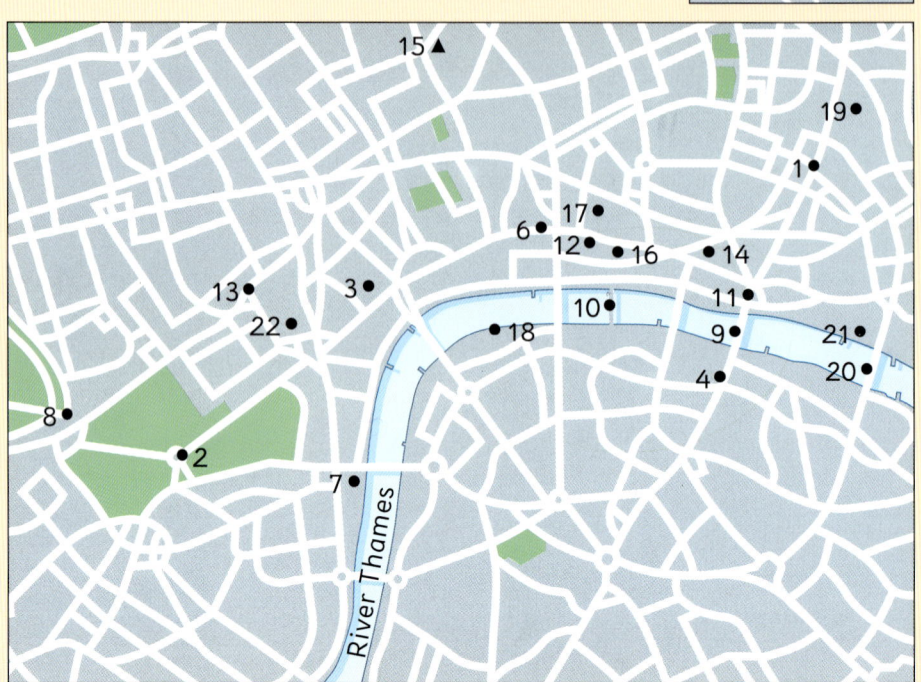

At the movies

The Adventures of Sherlock Holmes.
Directed by Alfred Werker, 1939.

Oliver Twist.
Directed by David Lean, 1948.

101 Dalmatians.
Directed by Stephen Herek, 1996.

Parent Trap.
Directed by Nancy Meyers, 1998.

On the Internet

Take a virtual bus tour around London:
www.bbc.co.uk/london/panoramics/bus_tour.shtml

More about the Great Fire of London:
www.channel4.com/history/microsites/H/history/fire

Find out more about the lives of children during World War II at:
www.bbc.co.uk/history/ww2children/

Find out more about the Royal Family at:
www.royal.gov.uk/output/Page266.asp

Find out more about London's bridges at:
www.bbc.co.uk/london/panoramics/bridges.shtml

GLOSSARY

advantage something useful or good

commemorate be made as a reminder of someone or something

commercial relating to trade

democracy the government of a country by electing representatives, called politicians, to make decisions about how the country is run

environmentally friendly not harmful to the natural environment

executed killed for committing crimes

fortress building that is protected against attack

infested having a lot of an unpleasant type of animal

merchants people who make money from buying and selling things

monarchy government or country ruled by a king or queen

monument building or statue made to remind people of a person or event

orphan child whose parents have died

parliament group of people who discuss issues relating to governing a country and bring about laws

pedestrians people who are walking

permanent intended to last

plague disease that spreads to many people and causes many deaths, in particular the bubonic plague and variations of it

plinth the lowest part of the base of a column, statue or wall

politician a person taking an active part in the way a country is run, especially as a representative in parliament

port town or city on the coast that is used for sea traffic

rebelling fighting against the people or group in charge

redeveloped having buildings knocked down and new ones built in their place

sacked having things of value stolen or destroyed

sewer pipe or channel to carry sewage

Swinging Sixties name given to the fashion and music scene of the 1960s

INDEX

Big Ben 28, 29
Bishopsgate 10, 11
Black Death 5
Blitz 4, 20–21
bombs 20, 21
bridges 4, 5, 16–17
   London Bridge 4, 16, 17
   Millennium Bridge 16, 17
   Tower Bridge 16, 17
Buckingham Palace 18–19
buses 10, 11

cafés 26, 27
carriages, horse-drawn 11
Cheapside 7
Crown Jewels 19

executions 23

George Inn 28, 29
Globe Theatre 27
Great Fire of 1666 4, 8–9
Great Plague 5
Greenwich 7

High Holborn 10, 11
Hook, Robert 8
Houses of Parliament 4, 5, 28–29
Hyde Park Corner 24–25

laws 13
London Underground 20

maps 5, 30
markets 12–13
   Covent Garden 26–27
   Smithfield Market 12, 13
   Spitalfields Market 12, 13
memorials 8–9, 25
merchants 10
Midland Grand Hotel 28
Millennium Dome 5
Monument 8–9

Newgate Gaol 22–23

Old Bailey 22–23

Palace of Westminster 28–29
Pepys, Samuel 9
Piccadilly 4
pollution 5, 11
ports 14
prisons 14, 22–23
Pudding Lane 8

River Thames 4, 14–15, 17
Romans 4, 10
Royal Family 4, 18–19
Royal Festival Hall 26

Saxons 4
St Mary le Bow 6–7
St Pancras 28, 29
St Paul's Cathedral 20, 21
Shakespeare, William 27
ships 14, 15
shops 7, 12
South Bank 26–27
statues 9, 25
   Statue of Justice 22
Swinging Sixties 5

Tate Modern 27
tourists 15, 18, 19, 24
Tower of London 14, 15, 19
traders 12
Trafalgar Square 24–25
   Nelson's Column 24
traffic 11, 17

Vikings 4

Webb, Sir Ashton 18
West India Dock 14, 15
World War II 4, 20–21
Wren, Sir Christopher 8